Poem of the Week

Initial Consonants and a Sprinkling of Vowels

Betsy Franco

A Teaching Resource Center Publication

Published by
Teaching Resource Center
P.O. Box 82777
San Diego, CA 92138

Project Editor–Anne Linehan
Edited by Laura Woodard
Design and production by Janis Poe
Illustrations by Linda Starr

Printed in the United States of America
ISBN: 1-56785-042-1

Acknowledgements

For James, Tom, Davy,
and the children at El Carmelo School,
whose thoughts, dreams, struggles,
and adventures inspired these poems

Choosing Poems

You're free to use the poems in any order that suits you. If you introduce the consonants one by one, you're ready. If you present a letter a week, you're set. Even if you're on a year-round schedule, there are enough poems for you.

In the chart that follows, the poems have been organized by initial consonants and vowels. Most consonants have two poems. The least frequently used consonants (Q, V, X, Y, Z) and the vowels each have one poem.

Table of Contents

Teacher Notes

Use *Poem of the Week* to share the rhythm and cadence of poetry and the joy of poetic language with the children in your class. The topics of the poems were selected to reflect a child's world, making this book a natural, weekly link to the family. And if you choose, you can use each poem as the context for raising phonemic awareness and inspiring creativity.

Overview

Poetry is a mainstay in the primary classroom. But it's usually up to you to beg, steal, or borrow the poems you need. It's usually your job to find poetry that's relevant, lively, touching, and phonetically appropriate.

Relax. The poems are written. There's one poem per week, and there's also a bonus. Since phonemic awareness is coming into such sharp focus, each poem highlights a particular initial consonant. (The final poems highlight an initial vowel.)

If you choose, you can follow the suggestions that accompany each poem. That way, you can enjoy the poetry with your children, while at the same time introducing, teaching, or reviewing the featured consonant. The suggestions will help you make the poems interactive as well.

Along with the poems and suggestions, we've provided strips for each poem that fit into the Desktop Pocket Chart. With all these tools, groups can enjoy the poems, individual children can learn from and elaborate on the poems, and you can relax and enjoy your teaching.

Versatility Plus

You can choose poems by:
- theme
- week
- phonemic focus
- your particular interests

What You've Got

- a poem for every week of the year
- suggestions on how to work with the consonant emphasized in each poem
- suggestions for making the poems personal and interactive for the children
- poetry strips and an illustration that fit into the Desktop Pocket Chart

Desktop Pocket Chart
12"wide x 16"high, 10 pockets

Useful Accessories

The following accessories can be useful when extending the poems:

Desktop Pocket Chart

Poem of the Week includes strips for each poem that fit into the 12" x 16" Desktop Pocket Chart. You can use the poems for intimate group work with the help of this miniature pocket chart.

Word Builder Kit

This kit includes letter holders and laminated letters to help children stay organized as they build words and work with consonants.

Magic Wand

A Magic Wand can be truly magical when pointing out onsets and rimes and other phonemic elements in the poems. If you don't have the official Magic Wand, use the pattern on page 9 to create one.

Wikki Stix

Made of waxed yarn, Wikki Stix temporarily stick to almost any surface, including the student poem and the Desktop Pocket Chart. They are perfect for underlining or circling the phonemic elements or the rhyming words in the poems.

Highlighter Tape

This removable, colorful, transparent tape can be used to highlight words, phonemic elements, or phrases on the Desktop Pocket Chart.

Sticky Notes

Sticky notes are useful for making poems interactive by covering and replacing words on the Desktop Pocket Chart.

Standard Pocket Chart and Sentence Strips

If you choose to, you can reproduce the poems on standard pocket chart strips for whole class or group instruction.

Student Poems

For every week of the year, you have a poem, enlarged for easy reading. You can make a copy of the poem for each child, leaving off the Suggestions for Going Further.

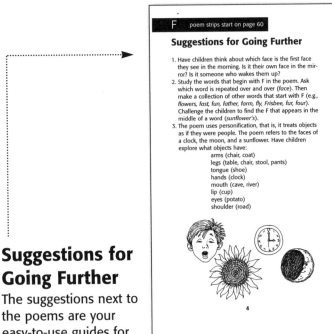

F   poem strips start on page 60

Suggestions for Going Further

1. Have children think about which face is the first face they see in the morning. Is it their own face in the mirror? Is it someone who wakes them up?
2. Study the words that begin with F in the poem. Ask which word is repeated over and over (*face*). Then make a collection of other words that start with F (e.g., *flowers, fast, fun, father, farm, fly, Frisbee, fur, four*). Challenge the children to find the F that appears in the middle of a word (*sunflower's*).
3. The poem uses personification, that is, it treats objects as if they were people. The poem refers to the faces of a clock, the moon, and a sunflower. Have children explore what objects have:
   arms (chair, coat)
   legs (table, chair, stool, pants)
   tongue (shoe)
   hands (clock)
   mouth (cave, river)
   lip (cup)
   eyes (potato)
   shoulder (road)

Faces

A clock has a face.

The moon has a face.

A sunflower's face is yellow.

The first face

that I see each day

is a very sleepy fellow!

4

Suggestions for Going Further

The suggestions next to the poems are your easy-to-use guides for extending the poems, if the ideas suit your needs. The suggestions point out the consonants in the poems and how to make use of them. The suggestions also include ideas for extending the poems and making them interactive and personal for the children.

Strips for the Desktop Pocket Chart

You're all set for group work. By copying and cutting out the enlarged strips (starting on page 52) and using them in the Desktop Pocket Chart, you can display a poem for many eyes to see. Groups of children can interact with the poem in this intimate, yet practical medium. Use index tag when copying for sturdier strips.

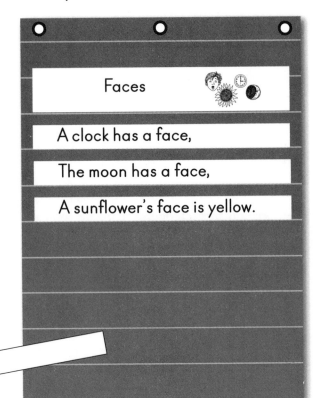

Faces

A clock has a face,

The moon has a face,

A sunflower's face is yellow.

The first face

that I see each day

is a very sleepy fellow!

How to Use the Elements of the Book

There are many ways to use *Poem of the Week.* You can copy the student poems for individual use. You can reconstruct the poem on a Desktop Pocket Chart for group work. You can make your own strips for a Standard Pocket Chart.

Ways to Use the Student Poems

- Read through and select the poem that suits your needs.
- Fill in any blanks or add blanks to the poem, if you choose.
- Make a copy of the poem without the Suggestions. Or cut out the poem and adhere it to the center of another paper before copying.
- Enjoy the poem for the beauty of the words, the rhythm, and the content.
- Have each child add the poem to a personal poetry anthology.
- Follow the Suggestions for Going Further that make sense to you.
- Send poem books home to be shared with family members.

Going Further with the Student Poems

→ Make the poems interactive. Give children a chance to personalize the poem by creating a blank for them to fill with their own words. It's as simple as whiting out or taping over a word or phrase in the student poem before making copies.

Lenny's Losing Streak

Lenny lost his _____.

Lenny lost his lock.

Lenny lost his _____

and his lollipop.

Lenny lost his licorice

and money for the week.

Lenny seems to be

on a losing streak!

→ Let children illustrate the poem or make an appropriate border for it.

Froggy's Morning Swim
A True Story

A little frog was doing laps
in the baby wading pool.
Frog kick, frog kick, glide, glide.
That fine little frog was cool.

I caught him in my fingers
but he flipped and flopped back in.
The baby pool was a perfect place
for froggy's morning swim.

Riding, Rolling, Rowing

R̲iding

    on an ocean wave,

R̲olling

    down a grassy hill,

R̲owing

    on a R̲iver R̲aft,

R̲eally

    can be such a thrill!

← White out or tape over consonants in the poem, and let children fill them in.

↓ Have children circle or under-line the particular consonant featured in the poem.

→ Add new verses or write variations on the poem using poetry frames.

↓ Make a sentence with alliteration using the words in the poem.

If I had a kingdom,

If I were king,

We'd h̲ave recess all day.

A D̲aring D̲ive

Someday I'll d̲o

a *DARING D̲IVE!*

Yes, any d̲ive

at all.

But since

I d̲on't know

how to d̲ive,

I'll d̲o a

CANNONBALL!

Little Holly has to wear a hat to hide her hairdo because she gave herself a horrible haircut.

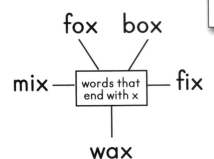

← Make lists or webs of words that share the consonant that is emphasized in the poem.

Ways to Use the Desktop Pocket Chart

• Copy the poetry strips and the illustration onto index tag.
• Cut out the strips and the illustration.
• Reconstruct the poem in the Desktop Pocket Chart. We've numbered each
  line to minimize confusion. You can keep the numbers or cut them off.
• Gather a group of children to recite the poem together and enjoy its rhythm.
• Work with the poem's phonemic focus in a relevant context.

Going Further with the Desktop Pocket Chart

• Use non-permanent markers, Wikki Stix, or highlighting tape to highlight phonemes on the pocket chart strips.
• Let children use a pointer such as a Magic Wand to identify particular consonants or rhyming words.

• Use sticky notes to cover words in the poem. Let children suggest new words to write in their place to personalize or change the poem. Alternatively, you can use blank word cards made from heavy paper to cover and replace words. (Cards should be about 2" long and 1" high.)

• Cover phrases in the poem with blank strips and let children interact with the poem by rewriting the phrases. (Strips should be about 1" high.)

Muddy mud,

Puddly mud,

Splashing in the yucky mud,

Messing up your shoes

with slime.

Having a marvelous

muddy time!

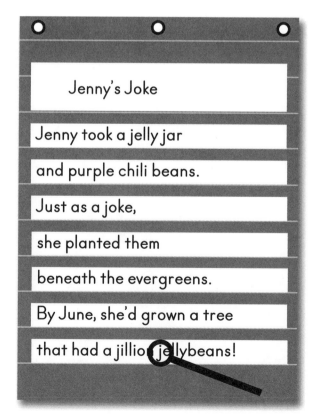

Jenny's Joke

Jenny took a jelly jar

and purple chili beans.

Just as a joke,

she planted them

beneath the evergreens.

By June, she'd grown a tree

that had a jillion jellybeans!

Sammy's Constellation

Kayla cut out

sixteen stars

and stuck them

to the sky,

to make a constellation

of her best friend Ali

7

→ Have children use letters to build banks of words that share the same consonant as the one featured in the poem.

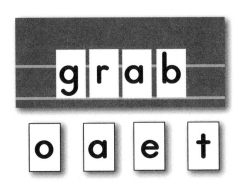

↓ Use chart paper to create banks or webs of words with the same consonant element as the poem.

W Words in the Poem	Other W Words
when	wall
Walter	walk
watermelon	wash
war	wig
was	win
were	wish
watered	week
winter	went
warm	wet
we	work

→ Create puzzle cards by leaving off the key consonant in words from the poem and have children figure out the mystery words.

Y words

___ ak

___ aks

___ ard

___ et

___ ell

___ ip

→ Make a word problem from the poem.

↓ Make word cards focusing on the consonant from the poem, and let children sort the cards in different ways.

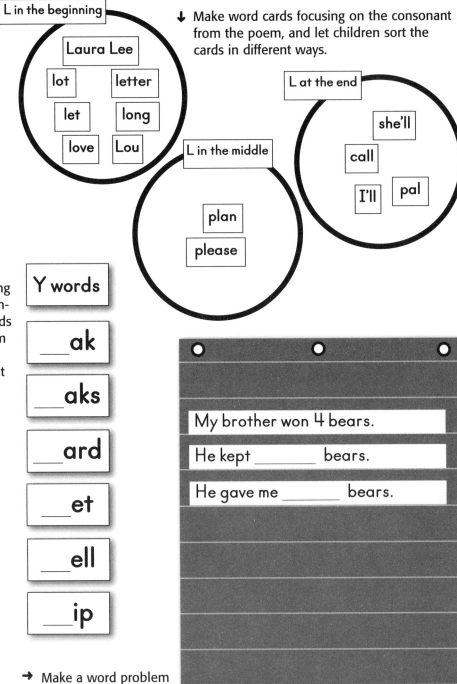

Magic Wand Pattern

Copy the wand onto index tag and cut it out.
Trace the wand pattern onto cardboard and cut it out.
Glue the index tag wand to the cardboard wand.
Decorate the wand with colored markers, sequins, ribbons, and glitter.

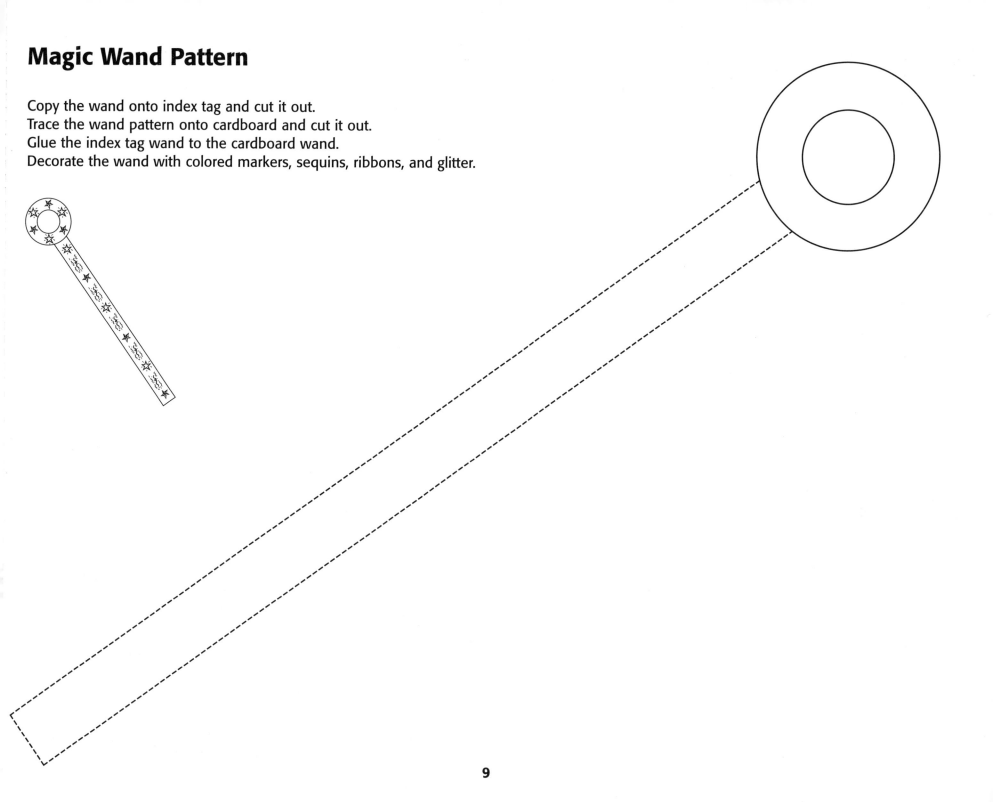

Suggestions for Going Further

1. Discuss the title. Ask if children have ever won a prize at a fair or amusement park. Talk about the games at a fair that offer stuffed animals for prizes.
2. Let the children be "B" detectives. Make the Magic Wand into a magnifying glass (like Sherlock Holmes'). Let children take turns finding the B words in the poem in the Desktop Pocket Chart. Highlight the words in the poetry strips using markers, Wikki Stix or highlighter tape. Ask which two B words are used the most (*brother, bear*).
3. Encourage children to be creative. Let them change the poem in many different ways:
   • *Brother* can be changed to *sister.*
   • The color *brown* can be a different color.
   • The word *bear* can be replaced by another stuffed animal that starts with the letter B (e.g., *bulldog, bird, buffalo, brontosaurus*).
4. Make the poem into a problem solving situation. Create bears for the pocket chart. Then have the children divide the bears equally (or unequally) between both brothers. For example, make it four bears and let the children give two to each brother. Write the problem on the Desktop Pocket Chart.

My brother won 4 bears.
He kept ____ bears.
He gave me ___ bears.

FIRST PRIZE

Bears at the Fair

My brother won
a bear that's brown.
My brother won
a bear that's blue.
My brother gave
one bear to me,
because he never
needed two!

Suggestions for Going Further

1. Set the scene before reading the poem. (The narrator sleeps in the bottom bunk of a bunk bed.) Ask how many children in your class sleep in a bunkbed.
2. Ask children to find all the words that begin with the letter B and underline them on the student poem. Make a "B tree" on chart paper.
   If children read the previous B poem, ask which B words are repeated in this poem (*bear, brother*). (Note that the brothers in this poem could be the same as those in the previous poem.) Ask children which two words have a B sound in the middle of the word (*remembers, above*).

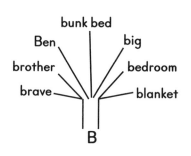

3. Put all the B words on word cards and invite children to sort them. Words can be sorted by the position of the B in the word, by the number of letters in the word, and by the first two letters of the word.
4. Make a class graph about brothers. The categories can be:
   I have a big brother.
   I have a little brother.
   I don't have any brothers.
   The same graph can be made about sisters.

Brave in the Bedroom

Below in the bunkbed
Ben sleeps every night.
He pulls up his blanket
and hugs his bear tight.

And when he remembers
his big brother Dave
is right up above him,
it makes him feel brave!

Suggestions for Going Further

1. There are many C words in the poem. Have children identify the C words on the Desktop Pocket Chart with the Magic Wand or another pointer. Highlight all the C's using marker, Wikki Stix, or highlighter tape. Then make a list of the C words on chart paper. Ask if the children can find the C word that is used the most (*coins*).
2. Clap to the rhythm of the poem. This chant-like poem could even be used as a jump rope rhyme.
3. Help the children personalize the poem on the Desktop Pocket Chart. Leave off *cookie jar* in line 2 and *a hundred* in line 3. Have children think of different containers for keeping the coins (e.g., sock, tin can, glass jar) and different amounts of coins that could have been collected so far (e.g., fifty, one thousand, ten thousand).
4. Ask what kind of coins Cass is collecting. (Since they are copper, they must be pennies.) Provide real coins for the children to study. Compare the color of a penny to the color of the other coins.

Coin Collection

Cass collects coins
in a cookie jar.
She has a hundred coins
so far.
She counts her copper coins
with care.
Someday she'll be
a millionaire!

Suggestions for Going Further

1. Make sure children understand the words *stressed* and *calmly.* After reading the poem, highlight all the C words on the Desktop Pocket Chart. Children can point out the C with the Magic Wand and say the word aloud.
2. Write the C words on blank cards and sort them.

begins with C	has a C in the middle	has a C at the end
cat	across	Mac
collie		
can		
calmly		

3. On the Desktop Pocket Chart, cover the word *play* with a sticky note. Have children brainstorm other words that would fit, and write them in place of *play* (e.g., *run, roam, climb, purr, catch birds, catch mice, sleep*).
4. Look at the opposite words in the poem: *stressed* and *calm(ly).* Have children brainstorm other words that are opposites (e.g., *night/day, asleep/awake, up/down, big/small*).

13

Mac the Cat

With collie dogs
across the street,
my old cat Mac
was always stressed.

But then the collies
moved away.
Now Mac can calmly
play and rest.

Suggestions for Going Further

1. Talk about what a cannonball is and how it makes a big splash.
   Have children pantomime the poem, acting as if they're going to dive and then holding their legs as if doing a cannonball.

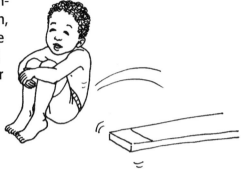

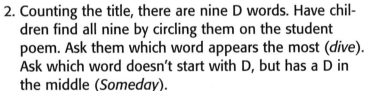

2. Counting the title, there are nine D words. Have children find all nine by circling them on the student poem. Ask them which word appears the most (*dive*). Ask which word doesn't start with D, but has a D in the middle (*Someday*).

3. Encourage children to think of something exciting or daring they would like to be able to do someday. Brainstorm some possibilities with the children (e.g., climb a mountain, fly a plane, go in a hot-air balloon, ride in a rocket ship, go surfing, ride an elephant, be a rock star, sing or dance in front of an audience, be a movie star, be an Olympic gymnast, put out fires). Then have the children copy the following sentence frame, fill in the blank, and illustrate what they've written (or dictated):

Someday I would like to be able to _____.

A Daring Dive

Someday I'll do
a *DARING DIVE!*
Yes, any dive at all.
But since
I don't know
how to dive,
I'll do a
CANNONBALL!

Suggestions for Going Further

1. Many of the D words in the poem are repeats.
   Challenge children to find:
   - how many times the word *dragon* or *dragons* is used (five in all)
   - how many times the word *dress* or *dressed* is used (two in all)
   - other D words in the poem (*dodging, Day, did*)
2. Talk about how Chinese New Year is celebrated. (People dress up in a dragon costume and dance through the streets.) Make a long dragon for display. Have the children decorate a square by writing a D word in large letters and decorating the word and the rest of the square. The finished squares can be lined up for the body. The head and tail can be added. See page 107 for the dragon blackline. You can display the poem beneath the dragon.

Chinese Dragons

Dragons, dragons
everywhere!
Dragons dodging
here and there.
Children dressed
in dragon dress.
It's New Year Day!
How did you guess?

Suggestions for Going Further

1. Have children think about which face is the first face they see in the morning. Is it their own face in the mirror? Is it someone who wakes them up?
2. Study the words that begin with F in the poem. Ask which word is repeated over and over (*face*). Then make a collection of other words that start with F (e.g., *flowers, fast, fun, father, farm, fly, Frisbee, fur, four*). Challenge the children to find the F that appears in the middle of a word (*sunflower's*).
3. The poem uses personification, that is, it treats objects as if they were people. The poem refers to the faces of a clock, the moon, and a sunflower. Have the children explore what objects have:

        arms (chair, coat)
        legs (table, chair, stool, pants)
        tongue (shoe)
        hands (clock)
        mouth (cave, river)
        lip (cup)
        eyes (potato)
        shoulder (road)

Faces

A clock has a face.

The moon has a face.

A sunflower's face is yellow.

The first face

that I see each day

is a very sleepy fellow!

Suggestions for Going Further

1. Have children work in partners to make a web of the words in the poem that have the letter F. Ask if they found the only word that has an F in the middle (*perfect*).

```
              flopped
  flipped              Froggy's
            ┌─────┐
            │  F  │
  fingers   └─────┘   perfect
        fine     frog
```

2. Let pairs of children act out the poem as it is read.
3. Ask children to illustrate the poem and write about their picture, using at least two words that contain the letter F.

Froggy's Morning Swim
A True Story

A little frog was doing laps
  in the baby wading pool.
Frog kick, frog kick, glide, glide.
  That fine little frog was cool.

I caught him in my fingers
  but he flipped and flopped back in.
The baby pool was a perfect place
  for froggy's morning swim.

G poem strips start on page 62

Suggestions for Going Further

1. Let children highlight the hard G words on the poem in the Desktop Pocket Chart using markers, Wikki Stix or highlighter tape. Emphasize those words as you read the poem aloud a second time. Talk about the word *giraffe*. It stands out in the poem because it starts with a G but it has the soft G sound.
2. Pass out Word Builder Kits (or homemade word builders), and have children create one-syllable G words (e.g., *go, get, got, grab, great, gate, guts*).
3. Time to be creative. Ask children to draw a picture of Greg the Giraffe. Have them include Greg's autograph at the bottom of the picture. Then have the children practice their own signatures, and collect each other's autographs.

18

The Autograph of a Giraffe

The autograph of a giraffe
is a very hard thing to get.
You've got to grab
her great, long neck
and go to the top
to get it all set.
And if she agrees,
then grab your hat,
for sliding down
is your best bet.

Suggestions for Going Further

1. Have children create cards for the hard G words. These words can be nicely sorted according to different criteria. For example, they can be sorted by the first two (or three) letters or by the number of letters in the word:

gr	gl	goo	go
gray	glasses	googly	got
green		goofy	
great			

2. Declare a "Sunglasses Day." You can have children make sunglasses using the template on page 108. Have children cut the front of the glasses out of different colored construction paper and the sides of the glasses out of tagboard. Colored cellophane can be taped on for the lenses. Make a class graph of the glasses showing how many children chose each color.

19

Glasses

Gray glasses,
Green glasses,
Glasses that shine.
Goofy glasses,
Great glasses,
Glasses so fine.
Googly glasses,
Dark glasses, in the sunshine.
I can see a whole lot more,
now that I've got mine.

Suggestions for Going Further

1. Talk about hummingbirds (or "hummers") together:
   - They are very small birds.
   - They can fly very quickly and can dart about in all directions.
   - Hummingbirds are attracted to feeders that contain sugar water.
   - To attract hummingbirds, you can plant a garden with trumpet-shaped flowers. They especially like the color red.
   - Hummingbirds suck the nectar out of flowers with their long, narrow beaks.
2. This poem has H words of many different lengths. Challenge children to find H words with:

   three letters (*his*)
   four letters (*head, home*)
   five letters (*happy*)
   six letters (*headed, hummer*)

   Ask how many letters in the word hummingbird (eleven). Brainstorm other H words as a class.
3. Have children draw a picture of a hummingbird garden with the baby hummingbird in it. Encourage each child to write or dictate a sentence about the little hummingbird under his or her picture.

The Baby Hummingbird
A True Story

The hummingbird
was happy
with a flower
that was red.
But when the hummer
headed home,
the bud was
on his head!

Suggestions for Going Further

1. Have children circle all the H words on the student poem. Then write the words on blank word cards. Arrange the cards in different ways, and work together to make a sentence (or two) with *alliteration* (repeating the same initial sound), using as many of the words as possible. Example: *Little Holly has to wear a hat to hide her hairdo because she gave herself a horrible, hilarious haircut.*

2. Play around with the words in the poem:
   • On the Desktop Pocket Chart poem, cover the rhyming words with sticky notes. Let the children figure out which words are missing.
   • Cover the word *hilarious* and let children find other words to replace it (e.g., *silly, bad, horrible, wacky, ridiculous, funny*).
   • Let children substitute other words for *baseball hat* (e.g., *baseball cap, winter hat, bike helmet, sweatshirt hood, cowboy hat, ski cap, straw hat*).

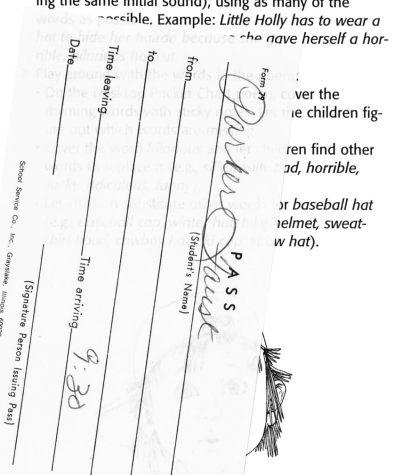

The Horrible, Hilarious Haircut

Little Holly Hollenback
had long and curly hair.

But she gave herself a haircut
and her head is nearly bare.

The hairdo looks hilarious—
She hardly seems to care.

But she'd better wear her baseball hat
to hide her silly hair.

Suggestions for Going Further

1. As the children read through the poem on the Desktop Pocket Chart, let them take turns identifying the J words using the Magic Wand. Make puzzle cards for the words they find, leaving out the initial consonant:

   ___ust   ___og
   ___olly   ___okes
   ___uggle

   Let children take turns reading the puzzle cards. Then add other puzzle cards:

   ___am   ___ump
   ___ar   ___eep
   ___et   ___ob
   ___ug   ___unk

2. If children are ready for this step, ask which two words start with the J sound but don't begin with the letter J (*giant, gentle*).
3. Invite children to be authors. Let them complete the following frame:

   If I just knew a giant, he'd (or she'd) _____.
   If I just knew a giant, he'd (or she'd) _____.

If I Just Knew a Giant

If I just knew a giant
he'd jog me to school.
He'd be jolly and gentle,
and just plain cool.
If I just knew a giant,
he'd tell jokes all day,
and he'd juggle my friends,
in a very safe way.

Suggestions for Going Further

1. On the poetry strips in the Desktop Pocket Chart, highlight all the J words with markers, Wikki Stix or highlighter tape. Then read the poem as a class, with a special emphasis on those words.
2. Play with the words in the poem. Ask the children what other months start with J and could be substituted for *June* (*January, July*). Use sticky notes over the word *June* to make the substitution. Do the same with *a jillion.* Ask what other numbers could be written in its place (*a thousand, a million, a billion*). Talk about the fact that a *jillion* isn't really a number.
3. Have children think about the compound word *starfish.* Invite them to write about how they could create a starfish from a star and a fish, the way Jenny made jellybeans from jelly and beans. Let them illustrate their words.

Jenny's Joke

Jenny took a jelly jar
and purple chili beans.
Just as a joke,
she planted them
beneath the evergreens.
By June, she'd grown a tree
that had a jillion jellybeans!

Suggestions for Going Further

1. Make sure the children understand what a kingdom is. When reading the poem, read through the verses and repeat the first verse as a refrain.
2. It's time to be word detectives. List all the K words in the poem (*kingdom, king, kitten, kites, kick*). Ask the children to figure out what is the same about all of them. (They all start with *ki*.) Ask if they can think of some K words that don't start with *ki* (e.g., *kettle, key, kept, keeper, keg, Kool-Aid, kangaroo, karate, koala, kung fu*).
3. Let children use their imaginations to complete this frame:

   If I had a kingdom,
   If I were king,
   we'd _____ all day.

   Have children fill in one or more lines, depending on their abilities.

24

If I Had a Kingdom

If I had a kingdom
then I would be king.
Yes, I would be king
of everything!

We'd each have a kitten.
We'd fly lots of kites.
We'd kick around balls
and stay up most nights!

(Repeat first four lines.)

Suggestions for Going Further

1. Challenge children to find all the words that contain the letter K. Write them on cards, and let the class sort them in different ways. Words can be sorted by the location of the K (as shown below), or by the number of letters in the word.

K in the beginning	K at the end
kissed	milk
kitten	dark
Kay	
kept	

   Ask if the children can find the word in the poem that has the same sound as K but doesn't start with a K (*climbed*).

2. Make a silly version of the poem using the Desktop Pocket Chart. Substitute *koala* or *kangaroo* for *kitten.* Children will need to finish line 7 in a different way. Some examples:

   For the koala: He kept cuddling and cuddling,
                           He kept climbing on the furniture,
   For the kangaroo: He kept jumping and jumping,

25

Kay's Kitten

Kay kissed her kitten
and put him to bed.
She gave him some milk
and rubbed his soft head.
But when it got dark,
he climbed in with Kay.
He kept purring and purring,
till Kay let him stay.

Suggestions for Going Further

1. Lenny was on a real losing streak! Let children make a list of everything Lenny lost. Children can add other things Lenny might have lost that begin with the letter L (or have the letter L in the middle or end). Some examples:

L in the beginning	L in the middle	L at the end
liver	milk	pill
lead pencil	silk	bill
leopard	belt	grill
lemon	clam	ball
lawn mower	clown	doll
ladybug		bell
lily		
llama		
letter		

2. Substitute some of the words above for the words *lunch box, lizard,* and *licorice* to create a new, and probably funny, version of the poem.
3. Substitute *found* for *lost* and *finding* for *losing.*

Lenny's Losing Streak

Lenny lost his lunch box.
Lenny lost his lock.
Lenny lost his lizard
and his lollipop,
Lenny lost his licorice
and money for the week.
Lenny seems to be
on a losing streak!

L poem strips start on page 74

Suggestions for Going Further

1. There are lots of L words in the poem. Some words have the L in the beginning of the word, some in the middle, and some at the end.

beginning	middle	end
Laura Lee	plan	she'll
lot	please	call
letter		pal
let		I'll
long		
love		
Lou		

   Put the words on cards. Sort them by position in the word, as shown above.

2. Provide paper for children to write letters to each other. Explain that they can write about whatever they want. Tell them to ask for a letter in return, as Mary Lou did.

27

Dear Laura Lee,

How are you? I'm missing you a lot.
You had a lot to tell me
in the letter that I got.
My mother says she'll let me
call you in a week or two.
Please write a long, long letter,
and I'll try to write you, too.
I'd love to plan a visit.

   From your best pal, Mary Lou

Suggestions for Going Further

1. Find all the words that start with M by having children underline them on the student poem. Make puzzle cards for the words by leaving off the letter M:

   ___uddy   ___ud
   ___ucky   ___essy
   ___arvelous

2. Make puzzle cards for other M words as well.

   ___ad   ___ap
   ___at   ___en
   ___et   ___itt
   ___ix   ___itten
   ___unch   ___op

3. There are two words in the poem that have an M in the middle. Ask if the children can find *slime* and *jumping.*

4. Point out the *ing* endings in the poem. Then have the children rewrite the third and fifth lines, using an *ing* word to start. Examples:
   Splashing mud all over our clothes
   Rubbing mud on our arms and faces

28

Mucky Mud

Muddy mud,
   Puddly mud,
Jumping in the
   mucky mud.
Messing up your shoes
   with slime.
Having a marvelous
   muddy time!

Suggestions for Going Further

1. Let children take turns highlighting every M word on the student poem with marker or highlighter tape. Ask them how many words have the letter M. Let children pronounce them together. Ask if anyone found the word that has an M in the middle (*bump*).
2. What are some of the rules on the playground? Have each child or each pair of children contribute a rule to a class book. Each rule can be illustrated.
   Examples:
   No pushing on the slide.
   No tripping in soccer.
   No hogging the ball in basketball.
   Wait your turn in the jump rope line.

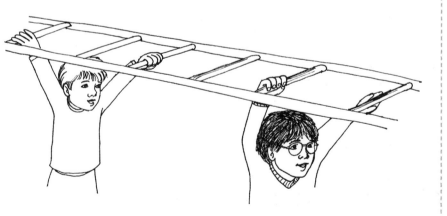

Manners on the Monkey Bars

Make room for Molly.
Watch out for Lars!
Don't mess around
on the monkey bars.
Your turn Marcy.
But don't bump Lars.
Mind your manners
on the monkey bars.

Suggestions for Going Further

1. Have the children find all the N words in the poem. Read it aloud, emphasizing the letter N. Make the poem sound like a tongue-twister.
2. Write all the N words on word cards and put them in a bag. Add some other easy words, too (e.g., *nag, nap, nest, net, nip, no, not,* and *nut*). Let the children take turns pulling a card from the bag and reading it aloud.
3. Be creative with the poetry strips in the Desktop Pocket Chart:
   • Substitute *nuts, peanuts,* or *chicken* for noodles.
   • Let children think of new words to replace *nibbles* (e.g., *gobbles, eats, munches*).

Nellie's Noodles

When Nellie eats noodles,
she's never, never neat.
But Norton her dog
stays underneath her feet.
He nibbles and nibbles
a nice noontime treat.
He vacuums up noodles
that she doesn't eat.

Suggestions for Going Further

1. This poem has many N's in the beginning, middle, and end of words. After children underline or highlight all the N words on the Desktop Pocket Chart, write them on word cards. The children can have fun sorting them into three yarn loops, according to the position of the N in the word. The word *noon* will present an interesting challenge.

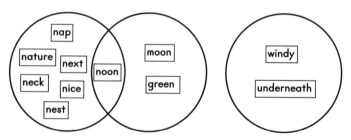

2. Napping in nature is a lovely topic for a class book. Children can create a page for the book by thinking of another place in nature that is good for napping (e.g., on a bed of clover, next to a pond or river, on newly-cut grass, in a meadow of wildflowers, in a rowboat on a lake, on a boulder warmed by the sun). Invite children to write a sentence and illustrate it for the book. I could nap _____.

Napping in Nature

Napping on a sandy beach,
Napping on the neck of a tree,

Napping next to a pond at noon,
Napping in a meadow green.

On a nice, warm, windy day,
In a nest of maple leaves,

Underneath the stars and moon,
Underneath a willow tree.

Suggestions for Going Further

1. Discuss what happens when someone eats a pink and purple popsicle. (His or her tongue, lips, and teeth can turn pink and purple. The popsicle can get drippy in the sun.)

2. The P's in this poem appear in unexpected locations in the words. Ask children to look closely at their student poems and underline all the P's–initial, medial, and final. Record their findings on chart paper. Then look at the words from other angles:
   • Talk about the rhyming words (*drips, lips, tips*). Where are the P's?
   • Ask which two words have two P's (*popsicle, drippy*).

3. Who says the popsicle has to be pink and purple? Tape over or white out the words *pink* and *purple* before copying the student poem. Let children choose different colors for the popsicle. They can fill in the blanks with two different colors and draw a picture to match.

4. As a class, use the Desktop Pocket Chart to change the word *popsicle* to *lollipop* in the first four lines of the poem. Explore the words *popsicle* and *lollipop*. The syllable *pop* comes at the beginning of one word and at the end of the other!

Pink and Purple Popsicle

Pink and purple tongue,
Pink and purple lips,
Pink and purple teeth,
Pink and purple drips.
My pink and purple popsicle
is drippy when it tips!

Suggestions for Going Further

1. Explore the P words in the poem using the Desktop Pocket Chart and the Magic Wand or another pointer.
   - Have children take turns pointing to a word in the poem that starts with P (*people, painting, pretty*). Record the words on chart paper.
   - Ask children to find words with P in the middle (*dimple, grandpa, happy*).
   - Ask which word has two P's (*happy*).
   - Count how many times the word *people* appears (five times, including the title).
2. Discuss the theme of the poem. Ask the children if they look or act like anyone in their family, or if they like to do some activity that another member of the family likes to do. Let the children fill in the poetry frame below and illustrate it.
   I _____
   like _____.

People Say

People say I'm good at painting –
like my father Perry.

People say I'm very pretty –
like my mother Mary.

People say I have a dimple –
like my grandpa Lee.

No matter what the people say –
I'm happy to be me.

Suggestions for Going Further

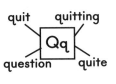

1. As a class, make a web of Q words on chart paper. Ask what children notice about all the Q words. (Every word begins with *qu*.)

2. Have children practice writing the capital and lower-case Q, since they are very different from each other. Ask where the capital Q appears in the poem and why. (*Quitting* and *Quite* are capitalized because they are in the title.)

3. Have each child inspect his or her fingernails and decide which is the longest nail (or which is his or her favorite nail if all are bitten). Make a graph of the results. Analyze the graph to find out which is the longest nail for the most children – thumb, pointer, middle, ring, or pinkie.

4. Provide a clock with movable hands and have children pick a different time of day in line 4.

I'm Quitting Quite Soon

I haven't quite quit
biting my nails,
but I'm thinking of
quitting at noon.

The question is, "Can I
quit biting my nails?"
The answer is: "Yes!
Quite soon!"

Suggestions for Going Further

1. After reading the poem, inspect it carefully for patterns. The first two lines in every verse are short lines and the third verse is a long line. All lines end with the word *rocks.*
2. List all the R words in the poem, including the title. Tally how many times the word *rocks* appears.

   rocks   𝍷𝍷𝍷𝍷𝍷 𝍷𝍷𝍷𝍷𝍷

3. Ask children to bring in rocks. Make labels and sort the rocks by different attributes. Some examples:
   • red rocks, white rocks, gray rocks
   • rough rock, smooth rocks
   • round rocks, rocks that aren't round
   • big rocks, small rocks

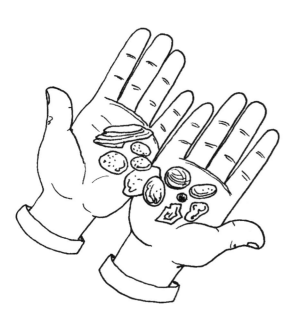

Cool Rocks

Flat rocks
Round rocks,
Skip-them-on-the-pond rocks.
Rough rocks,
Neat rocks,
Kick-them-down-the-street rocks.
Rare rocks
grand rocks
Hold-them-in-your-hand rocks!

Suggestions for Going Further

1. Let children discover that there's a pattern to the poem: every phrase starts with an R word that has an *ing* ending.
2. Have children underline all the R words on their student poems. (Don't forget *grassy* and *thrill!*) Then brainstorm more R words.
3. Lead a discussion about thrilling things children have already done (e.g., running down a steep hill, sliding down a long slide, going on a water slide, swimming in the ocean, climbing a tree, swinging really high on the swing, skateboarding, rollerblading, sailing a sailboat, riding in a motorboat, jumping on a trampoline). Invite them to complete the frame below and illustrate it. The phrase should start with an *ing* word.

_____ can be such a thrill!

Riding, Rolling, Rowing

Riding

   on an ocean wave,

Rolling

   down a grassy hill,

Rowing

   on a river raft,

Really

   can be such a thrill!

Suggestions for Going Further

1. Before reading the poem, it's helpful to tell children that *Si*, the last word in the poem, is short for *Simon.* The Hebrew name *Shai* (pronounced *Shy*) would work here as well. You might also want to talk about some of the well-known constellations, such as the *Big Dipper*, the *Little Dipper*, and *Orion.* You can show the children pictures of constellations from a book such as *Find the Constellations* by H.A. Rey (Houghton Mifflin, 1976).

2. Use the Desktop Pocket Chart to find all the S words, line-by-line. Some children will notice the S in the words *constellation*, *his*, and *best.* Write the S words on word cards and have children sort them by the position of the S in the word. Then line up the cards in order, according to the number of letters in each word.

   Si
   sky, his
   best
   stars, stuck,
   Sammy
   sixteen
   constellation

3. On the Desktop Pocket Chart, children can substitute their names for Sammy's and their friends' names for Si's.
   As a follow-up, have some fun with the idea of the poem. Let children design a constellation by drawing an object or person in pencil, sticking stars to the drawing, and erasing the pencil lines. Under the constellation, children can complete the following phrases:
   My constellation has ___ stars.
   It is a constellation of _____.

37

Sammy's Constellation

Sammy cut out
sixteen stars
and stuck them
to the sky,
to make a constellation
of his best friend Si.

Suggestions for Going Further

1. Put all the S words on word cards and have fun sorting them.
   - Find all the words that include the root word *sleep*.
   - Find all the words that are names.
   - Find all the words that begin with S, have an S in the middle, or have an S at the end.
   - Find the word with a double S.

Root Word Sleep	Name	Starts with S	Ends with S	Double S
sleep	Sally	she	things	messy
sleepover	Sara	super		
sleeping		stayed		
		seem		

2. Let children show off their talents as authors and illustrators, using the poem as inspiration. Have them complete one of the frames below and illustrate it:
   When a friend sleeps over, we like to _____
   or
   When a friend comes over, we like to _____

38

The Sleepover

Sally had a sleepover
with Sara and Kathleen.
She said they'd sleep
at ten o'clock
and keep things super clean.
But they were really messy
and they stayed up
through the night,
for sleeping at a sleepover
just didn't seem quite right.

Suggestions for Going Further

1. Make two lists of T words from the poem. Put proper names in one list and the remaining words in the other list. Have children discuss the difference in the lists. (All proper names are capitalized.)
2. Discuss the origins of the names that begin with T. (*Tomo* is a Japanese name; *Teresa* is a Mexican name.) Add other names that begin with T to the list. Encourage children to think of names from other cultures, such as *Tolu*, which is a Nigerian name. To help children brainstorm, ask them to think about names in their own families, names of neighbors, and names of children at the school. Substitute some new names in the first five lines of the poem.
3. Post a classroom list of children who can tie their own shoes. Have children add their names to the list when they have shown you that they have mastered this skill. There could also be lists for children who can recite their telephone numbers or addresses.

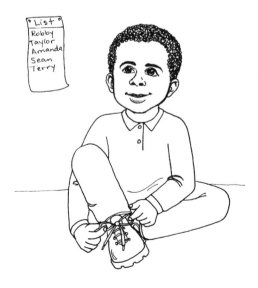

The List

Timmy can do it.

Tomo can do it.

Teresa can do it, too.

Teddy can do it.

Tina can do it.

and so can Terry Sue.

Hey, add my name

to the classroom list.

I learned to tie my shoe!

Suggestions for Going Further

1. Add to the fun of this poem by emphasizing its tongue-twister quality. The title and the second verse are especially tricky to say aloud.
2. On the poem strips in the Desktop Pocket Chart, have children highlight the T words with markers, Wikki Stix, or highlighter tape. Be sure children find all the words that have T in the middle or end. Then write the words on word cards and let the class sort them according to the position of the T in the word.

Beginning	Middle	End
tickly	spots	lot
ticklish	pits	got
tickle		best
ten		
toes		

2. Let children reveal their best tickle spots by copying and completing this sentence frame:

    My best tickly, ticklish tickle spot is my _____.

    Invite children to read their "tongue-twister" sentences aloud.

Tickly, Ticklish Tickle Spots

My chin, my pits,
my toes, my ribs —
I've got a lot
of tickle spots.

My ten little toes
are the best of the best
of the tickly tickle spots
I've got.

Suggestions for Going Further

1. Use the V words from the poem to start two lists: words with the V sound at the beginning and words with the V sound at the end. Then add to the lists.

V Sound at the Beginning	V Sound at the End
van	TV
videos	drive
vacation	dive
vein	five
very	save
vest	gave
vine	give
visit	hive
vote	love
Valentine	wave

2. Use sticky notes to cover the V words on the poetry strips in the Desktop Pocket Chart. Can the children tell you what the missing words are?

3. As a class, pack a van for a camping trip. What things would the children bring and what things would be left behind? Some examples:

Yes	No
tent	TV
sleeping bags	videos
pans	good clothes
matches	video games

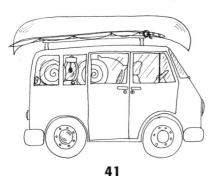

Pack the Van

Time for vacation.
Pack the van.
Drive all day.
That's the plan.

No videos.
No TV.
We're going camping
by the sea!

Suggestions for Going Further

1. Encourage children to act out the poem as it's read aloud, wiggling hands and fingers, and pantomiming the motions of making a snowball.
2. As a class, find the W words and make a list on chart paper. There are smaller W words inside these words. Challenge children to act as detectives and find them:

woolly   wool
wiggle   wig
winter   win
won't   won
warm   war

3. Have the children find the phrase that repeats in each verse (*I wiggle my . . .*).
   Then make up a new verse about feet and toes and build it in the Desktop Pocket Chart. Note that these new verses don't have to rhyme. For example:
   I wiggle my left foot,
   I wiggle my right,
   In warm winter socks
   so woolly and white.

   I wiggle my little toe
   I wiggle my big one,
   So out in the snow,
   my toes don't get numb.

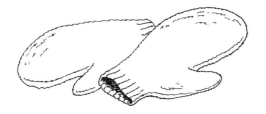

My Warm, Woolly, White, Winter Mittens

I wiggle my left hand,
I wiggle my right,
in warm winter mittens,
so woolly and white.

I wiggle my pinkie,
I wiggle my thumb,
so when I make snowballs,
my hands won't get numb.

Suggestions for Going Further

1. This poem is about a favorite children's pastime when watermelons are eaten outside–spitting the seeds. The poem is meant to be read at least two times in a row because of the cyclical nature of the subject matter. (The seeds that are left on the ground from the first seed–spitting war grow into new watermelons, and the children eat the new melons and have another seed-spitting war.)

2. Talk about other cycles: night and day, the seasons, the phases of the moon, the stages of a butterfly or frog.

3. Challenge children to find the W words in each sentence in the poem. Then brainstorm other W words.

W Words in the Poem	Other W Words
when	wall
Walter	walk
watermelon	wash
war	wig
was	win
were	wish
watered	week
winter	went
warm	wet
we	work

4. Have children build the one-syllable W words that they brainstormed using the Word Builder Kit (or a homemade word builder).

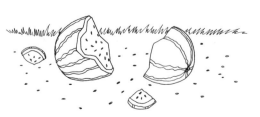

The Watermelon War

When Walter started a watermelon war,
   cleaning up seeds
   was quite a chore.
Some seeds were watered
   by the rain,
The winter, then the warm
   sun came.
New melons grew –
   we ate all four.
Then Walter started a watermelon war!

Suggestions for Going Further

1. X is an extraordinary letter. Using the poem in the Desktop Pocket Chart, let children point to the X words with the Magic Wand or another pointer.
2. Make webs of words that have X in different positions. Ask which web has the longest words and which has the shortest.

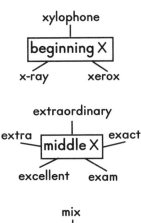

3. Let each child create an extra-special box by folding the box on page 109. Have the child write "My Extra-Special Box" on the top, along with his or her name. Small stones, feathers, beads, and other special things can be collected in the boxes.

44

My Extra-Special Box

A tiny shell,
A little fox,
a piece of wax
go in my box.

They're all mixed up
with beads and rocks
inside my
"extra-special" box.

Suggestions for Going Further

1. Invite the children to find all the Y words in the poem and list them on chart paper. Then create puzzle word cards. Children can take turns figuring out the Y word on each card and reading it aloud.
   ___ ak
   ___ aks
   ___ ard
   ___ et
   ___ ell
   ___ ip
2. On the Desktop Pocket Chart, replace the word *yak* with *giraffe, hippo, lion,* or the name of another wild animal. Read the poem again for a different, amusing effect.
3. Create a list of five wild animals the children think would make difficult pets—from skunks to grizzly bears. Let the children vote on which would be the most difficult pet, and make a graph of the results.

Do You Have a Yak Yet?

Yaks don't yip
and yaks don't yell.
Having a yak just might be swell.

But yaks need food
and a great big yard.
Yes, having a yak just might be hard.

If you don't have
a yak just yet,
You might want to get
a different pet!

Suggestions for Going Further

1. Read the poem in a fun way: read the first verse rapidly and the last verse very slowly.
2. Can children find the five Z words in the poem (including the title)? Start some Z trees with words from the poem and words from outside the poem. Each tree can focus on Z words with different vowels.
3. Choose another animal and have children analyze what it does and doesn't do by having children complete the following frame:
   A <u>bee</u> doesn't <u>growl</u>,
   but a <u>bee buzzes around.</u>

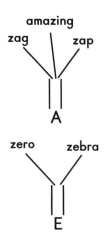

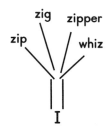

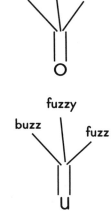

The Amazing Snail

A snail doesn't
whiz around,
or buzz around,
or zip around.

A snail crawls
in a nice slow way
and leaves a zigzag
on the ground.

Suggestions for Going Further

1. Create a hand shadow of an alligator using an overhead projector. Then read the poem aloud.
2. Underline the A words on the poetry strips in the Desktop Pocket Chart. Let the children use the Magic Wand to point to all the A words and read them aloud. Start a list of the words on chart paper, and encourage children to add to it.
3. Create other shadow animals (e.g., butterflies, dogs, rabbits). Challenge children to make animals that begin with A, such as ants, anteaters, armadillos, and arachnids (spiders).

47

Animal Shadows

An awesome,

angry,

alligator

showing

all her teeth.

With all

your fingers,

you can make

an animal

that's neat!

Suggestions for Going Further

1. Every line of the poem has an E word or two. Record the words as children find them. Ask how many times the word *eggs* appears (four times). Then let the children brainstorm more E words and record them (e.g., *egg rolls, earth, echo, every, each, easy, enormous, enemy, empty, enjoy, enough, escape*).
2. Have children use the words to make an E-filled sentence with alliteration.
   Example: *The enormous elephant enjoys eating eggs and egg rolls every day.*
3. As a class, write a new verse using *potatoes* instead of *eggs.*
   Example:
      Baked potatoes,
      Fried potatoes,
      Potatoes boiled through.
      I eat my potatoes with margarine,
      My pig does, too.
4. Write another version of the poem, substituting other E animals for the word *elephant.* Have children try *eagle, eel,* and/or *earthworm.*

Eggs

Fried eggs,
Scrambled eggs,
Eggs boiled through.
I eat my eggs with toast and milk.
My elephant does, too.

Suggestions for Going Further

1. Lots of repetition makes this poem fun to read. Have the children make a list of all the I words and keep a tally of how many times each appears in the poem (including the title). Don't forget *bigger*.

   Iggy   卌

   itty-bitty   ‖

   iguana   ‖

   isn't   ‖

   is |

   bigger |

2. Substitute other names for *Iggy* in the Desktop Pocket Chart (e.g., *Irving, Izzy, Isabelle, Iris, Inga, Itchy, Ivy, Irma, Isaac, Igbert*). Or try reading the poem aloud, substituting other I creatures for *Iggy the Iguana*. (Examples: *Irving the Inchworm, Izzy the Insect.*)

49

Itty-Bitty Iggy

Iggy the Iguana
should be bigger
by now.
But Iggy isn't growing
cuz he doesn't know how.
Iggy the Iguana
isn't big
as he should be.
But itty-bitty Iggy
is as cute as he can be.

O poem strips are on page 104

Suggestions for Going Further

1. This poem provides an opportunity to expand the children's vocabulary. There are some exciting words, short and long, and there are some words with the O hidden in the middle of the word. Ask children to underline the O words on the student poem.
   Beginning O: *old, only, Ollie, octopus, ordinary*
   Medial O: *not, looks, extraordinary*
   The words *okay* and *odd* aren't in the poem but they are fun O words to discuss.
2. On the Desktop Pocket Chart, have some fun by making substitutions. Replace the title and lines 3 and 4. Below are some ideas for lines 3 and 4, using other animals.
   When Ollie swings
   on his orangutan arms

   When Ollie runs
   on his ostrich legs

   When Ollie dives
   his otter dive

   When Ollie spreads
   his owl wings

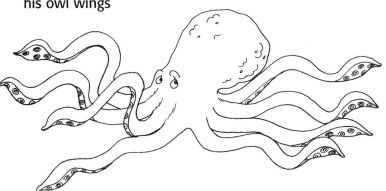

Old Ollie Octopus

Old Ollie is my only pet
and he's not ordinary.
When Ollie waves
his octopus arms,
he looks extraordinary.

Suggestions for Going Further

1. Use sticky notes to cover some of the U words on the poetry strips in the Desktop Pocket Chart (*under* in lines 1, 3, and 4, and some of the *ups.*) Let children tell you the words that are under the sticky notes.
2. U words can be interesting words: *under, up, umbrella, upset, upside-down, unwind.* Have the children write one of the words, illustrate it, and add their finished pages to a class book about the letter U.
3. Show the children another way to write the word *up*:

u^P

Then challenge the children to write the following U words in ways that reflect the meanings of the words: jump, buck, bump, dug, dunk, buzz, bus, hum, umbrella. Below are some possibilities.

$j^u mp$ $b^u ck$ $b^u mp$ bu^{zzzz}

$d_u g$ $d_u nk$ hummmmmmm

bus

Umbrella

Swimming Underwater

Under the water,

Underwater,

I can swim way under there,

And when I'm under

long enough,

then up, up, up

I'm ^{up} for air.

Poem Strip Contents

Note: Due to the requirements of our printer, the page numbers appear on the bottom strip on each page. To avoid confusion, we recommend that you make one copy and white out the page number before copying the poetry strips onto card stock.

Bears at the Fair

My brother won

a bear that's brown.

My brother won

a bear that's blue.

My brother gave

one bear to me,

8 because he never

9 needed two!

1 Brave in the Bedroom

2 Below in the bunkbed

3 Ben sleeps every night.

4 He pulls up his blanket

5 and hugs his bear tight.

54

And when he remembers

his big brother Dave

is right up above him,

it makes him feel brave!

Coin Collection

Cass collects coins

in a cookie jar.

She has a hundred coins

so far.

She counts her copper coins

with care.

Someday she'll be

a millionaire!

Mac the Cat

With collie dogs

across the street,

my old cat Mac

was always stressed.

But then the collies

moved away.

Now Mac can calmly

play and rest.

A Daring Dive

2 Someday I'll do

3 a *DARING DIVE!*

4 Yes, any dive at all.

5 But since

6 I don't know

7 how to dive,

I'll do a

CANNONBALL!

Chinese Dragons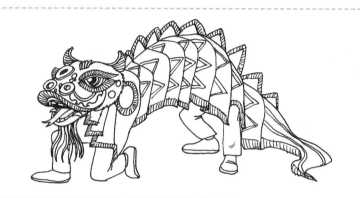

Dragons, dragons

everywhere!

Dragons dodging

here and there.

⁶ Children dressed

⁷ in dragon dress.

⁸ It's New Year Day!

⁹ How did you guess?

¹ Faces

² A clock has a face.

³ The moon has a face.

4 A sunflower's face is yellow.

5 The first face

6 that I see each day

7 is a very sleepy fellow!

1 Froggy's Morning Swim

A True Story

2 A little frog was doing laps

3 in the baby wading pool.

⁴ Frog kick, frog kick, glide, glide.

⁵ That fine little frog was cool.

⁶ I caught him in my fingers

⁷ but he flipped and flopped back in,

⁸ The baby pool was a perfect place

⁹ for froggy's morning swim.

¹ The Autograph of a Giraffe

The autograph of a giraffe

is a very hard thing to get.

You've got to grab

her great, long neck

and go to the top

to get it all set.

And if she agrees,

then grab your hat,

¹⁰ for sliding down

¹¹ is your best bet.

¹ Glasses

² Gray glasses,

³ Green glasses,

⁴ Glasses that shine.

⁵ Goofy glasses,

Great glasses,

Glasses so fine.

Googly glasses,

Dark glasses, in the sunshine.

I can see a whole lot more,

now that I've got mine.

The Baby Hummingbird
    A True Story

² The hummingbird

³ was happy

⁴ with a flower

⁵ that was red.

⁶ But when the hummer

⁷ headed home,

⁸ the bud was

⁹ on his head!

The Horrible, Hilarious Haircut

Little Holly Hollenback

had long and curly hair

But she gave herself a haircut

and her head is nearly bare.

The hairdo looks hilarious —

She hardly seems to care.

8 But she'd better wear her baseball ha

9 to hide her silly hair.

1 If I Just Knew a Giant

2 If I just knew a giant

3 he'd jog me to school.

4 He'd be jolly and gentle,

5 and just plain cool.

6 If I just knew a giant,

7 he'd tell jokes all day,

8 and he'd juggle my friends,

9 in a very safe way.

1

Jenny's Joke

2 Jenny took a jelly jar

3 and purple chili beans.

Just as a joke,

she planted them

beneath the evergreens.

By June, she'd grown a tree

that had a jillion jellybeans!

If I Had a Kingdom

If I had a kingdom

3 then I would be king.

4 Yes, I would be king

5 of everything!

6 We'd each have a kitten.

7 We'd fly lots of kites.

8 We'd kick around balls

9 and stay up most nights!

10 (Repeat first 4 lines)

Kay's Kitten

Kay kissed her kitten

and put him to bed.

She gave him some milk

and rubbed his soft head.

But when it got dark,

he climbed in with Kay.

He kept purring and purring,

till Kay let him stay.

Lenny's Losing Streak

Lenny lost his lunch box.

Lenny lost his lock.

Lenny lost his lizard.

and his lollipop,

Lenny lost his licorice

and money for the week,

Lenny seems to be

on a losing streak!

Dear Laura Lee,

How are you? I'm missing you a lot.

You had a lot to tell me

in the letter that I got.

My mother says she'll let me

call you in a week or two.

Please write a long, long letter,

and I'll try to write you, too.

I'd love to plan a visit.

From your best pal, Mary Lou

Mucky Mud

Muddy mud,

Puddly mud,

Jumping in the

mucky mud.

Messing up your shoes

with slime.

Having a marvelous

muddy time!

Manners on the
Monkey Bars

Make room for Molly.

Watch out for Lars!

Don't mess around

on the monkey bars.

6 Your turn Marcy.

7 But don't bump Lars.

8 Mind your manners

9 on the monkey bars.

1 Nellie's Noodles

2 When Nellie eats noodles,

3 she's never, never neat.

But Norton her dog

stays underneath her feet.

He nibbles and nibbles

a nice noontime treat.

He vacuums up noodles

that she doesn't eat.

Napping in Nature

Napping on a sandy beach,

Napping on the neck of a tree,

Napping next to a pond at noon,

Napping in a meadow green.

On a nice, warm, windy day,

In a nest of maple leaves,

Underneath the stars and moon,

Underneath a willow tree.

Pink and Purple Popsicle

Pink and purple tongue,

Pink and purple lips,

Pink and purple teeth,

Pink and purple drips.

My pink and purple popsicle

is drippy when it tips!

People Say

People say I'm good at painting —

like my father Perry.

People say I'm very pretty —

like my mother Mary.

People say I have a dimple —

like my grandpa Lee.

No matter what the people say —

I'm happy to be me.

I'm Quitting Quite Soon

I haven't quite quit

biting my nails,

but I'm thinking of

quitting at noon.

⁶ The question is, "Can I

⁷ quit biting my nails?"

⁸ The answer is: "Yes!

⁹ Quite soon!"

¹ Cool Rocks

² Flat rocks

³ Round rocks,

84

Skip-them-on-the-pond rocks.

Rough rocks,

Neat rocks,

Kick-them-down-the-street rocks.

Rare rocks

grand rocks

Hold-them-in-your-hand rocks!

Riding, Rolling, Rowing

Riding

on an ocean wave,

Rolling

down a grassy hill,

Rowing

on a river raft,

Really

can be such a thrill!

Sammy's Constellation

Sammy cut out

sixteen stars

and stuck them

to the sky,

6 to make a constellation

7 of his best friend Si.

1 The Sleepover

2 Sally had a sleepover

3 with Sara and Kathleen.

4 She said they'd sleep

5 at ten o'clock

and keep things super clean.

But they were really messy

and they stayed up through the night,

for sleeping at a sleepover

just didn't seem quite right.

The List

Timmy can do it.

3 Tomo can do it.

4 Teresa can do it, too.

5 Teddy can do it.

6 Tina can do it.

7 and so can Terry Sue.

8 Hey, add my name

9 to the classroom list.

10 I learned to tie my shoe!

Tickly, Ticklish Tickle Spots

My chin, my pits,

my toes, my ribs —

I've got a lot

of tickle spots.

My ten little toes

are the best of the best

of the tickly tickle spots

I've got.

1

Pack the Van

2 Time for vacation.

3 Pack the van.

4 Drive all day.

5 That's the plan.

No videos.

No TV.

We're going camping

by the sea!

My Warm, Woolly,

White, Winter Mittens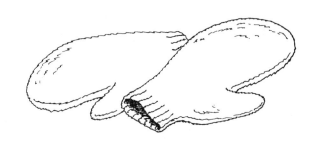

I wiggle my left hand,

I wiggle my right,

4 in warm winter mittens,

5 so woolly and white.

6 I wiggle my pinkie,

7 I wiggle my thumb,

8 so when I make snowballs,

9 my hands won't get numb.

1 The Watermelon War

When Walter started a watermelon war,

cleaning up seeds

was quite a chore.

Some seeds were watered

by the rain,

The winter, then the warm

sun came.

New melons grew —

we ate all four.

11 Then Walter started a watermelon war!

1 My Extra-Special Box

2 A tiny shell,

3 A little fox,

4 a piece of wax

5 go in my box.

They're all mixed up

with beads and rocks

inside my

"extra-special" box.

Do You Have a Yak Yet?

Yaks don't yip

and yaks don't yell.

4 Having a yak just might be swell.

5 But yaks need food

6 and a great big yard.

7 Yes, having a yak just might be hard.

8 If you don't have

9 a yak just yet,

10 You might want to get

11 a different pet!

The Amazing Snail

A snail doesn't

whiz around,

or buzz around,

or zip around.

A snail crawls

in a nice slow way

and leaves a zigzag

on the ground.

Animal Shadows

An awesome,

angry,

alligator

showing

6 all her teeth.

7 With all

8 your fingers,

9 you can make

10 an animal

11 that's neat!

Eggs

2 Fried eggs,

3 Scrambled eggs,

4 Eggs boiled through.

5 I eat my eggs with toast and milk.

6 My elephant does, too.

1 Itty-Bitty Iggy

2 Iggy the Iguana

should be bigger

by now.

But Iggy isn't growing

cuz he doesn't know how.

Iggy the Iguana

isn't big

as he should be.

But itty-bitty Iggy

⁹ is as cute as he can be.

¹ Old Ollie Octopus

² Old Ollie is my only pet

³ and he's not ordinary.

⁴ When Ollie waves

⁵ his octopus arms,

⁶ he looks extraordinary.

Swimming Underwater

Under the water,

Underwater,

I can swim way under there,

And when I'm under

long enough,

then up, up, up

I'm up for air.

The dragon below can be
colored and cut in half.
Any number of 3"x3" word cards
can be made to fill in the body.

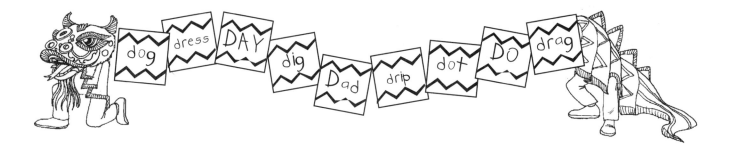

dog dress DAY dig Dad drip dot DO drag

Template for glasses.

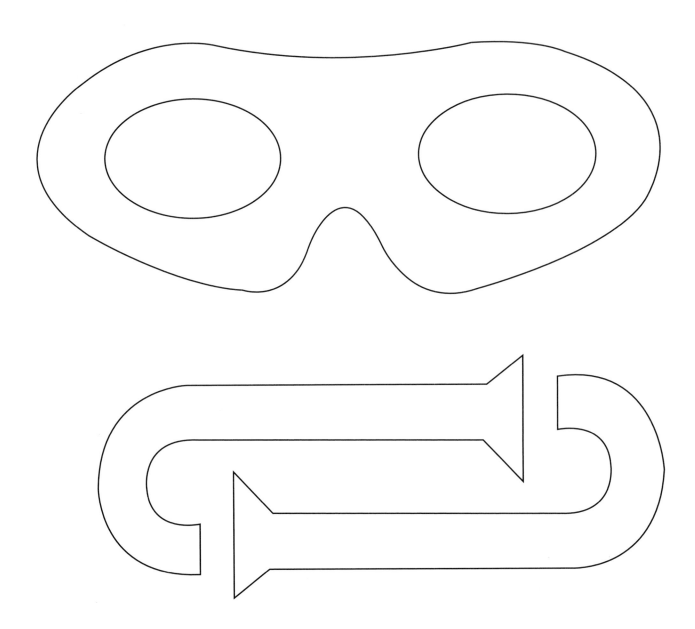

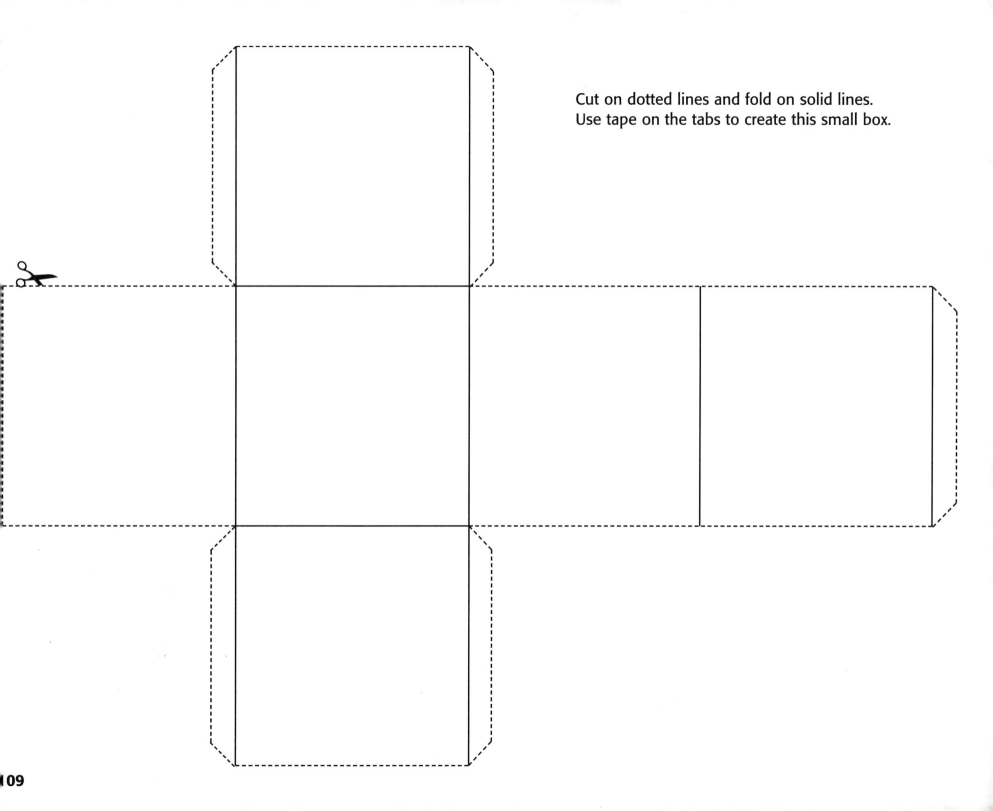

Cut on dotted lines and fold on solid lines.
Use tape on the tabs to create this small box.